27.00

Postal Workers

by Shannon Knudsen

Pull Ahead Books

Lerner Publications Company • Minneapolis

Lerner Publications Company
A division of Lerner Publishing Group
241 First Avenue North
Minneapolis, MN 55401 USA

Website address: www.lernerbooks.com

Words in **bold type** are explained in a glossary on page 31.

Library of Congress Cataloging-in-Publication Data

Knudsen, Shannon, 1971–
     Postal workers / by Shannon Knudsen.
       p.   cm. – (Pull ahead books)
     Includes index.
     ISBN-13: 978-0-8225-2846-3 (lib. bdg. : alk. paper)
     ISBN-10: 0-8225-2846-0 (lib. bdg. : alk. paper)
     1. Postal service–United States–Employees–Juvenile
literature. 2. Postal service–United States–Juvenile
literature. I. Title. II. Series.
HE6499.K59 2006
383'.4973'023–dc22   2005009028

Manufactured in the United States of America
1 2 3 4 5 6 – JR – 10 09 08 07 06 05

It's time to check the **mail**.

Did you get a letter? Who brought it to your mailbox?

Postal workers get our mail where it needs to go.

Every **community** has its own postal
workers. They do many different jobs.

A **letter carrier** drops off mail at people's homes and businesses. This is called **delivering** the mail.

The carrier also picks up mail that people want to send.

Some carriers work on foot. They carry
mail in a bag. Other carriers deliver
mail from a truck.

These carriers have delivered the day's mail. What happens to the mail that people want to send?

The carrier brings the mail to the
post office. Mail is sorted at the post
office so it can be sent to the
right places.

A **mail handler** takes the mail from the carrier. The handler checks to see if each piece of mail has a stamp.

What are stamps for?

Stamps pay for mail to be sent. People buy stamps at the post office and at other places.

Next, the mail handler feeds the
stamped letters into a machine. The
machine puts a mark over the stamp.
A marked stamp cannot be used again.

People also bring mail to the post office themselves.

A **clerk** takes the mail at a counter.

If the mail has no stamp, the clerk weighs the mail. She finds out how much it will cost to send. The sender pays the clerk.

What else do clerks do?

Clerks answer questions about mail.
They sell stamps too.

Next, workers feed all the mail into a
machine. The machine prints
a **bar code** on each piece of mail.

The bar code is printed on the bottom of the mail. It is made up of tiny lines. What do the lines mean?

BUSINESS REPLY MAIL
FIRST-CLASS MAIL   PERMIT NO. 309   HARLAN IA

POSTAGE WILL BE PAID BY ADDRESSEE

PO Box 5557
Harlan IA 51593-5057

18

The lines tell where the mail should be sent. A machine reads the bar codes on the mail. This machine sorts the mail into groups.

The groups of mail are placed in big trays, sacks, and bins.

Mail handlers use carts and tractors to move the mail to a loading dock.

The handlers load the mail onto trucks.
Truck drivers zoom away. Some mail
goes straight to another post office.

Other mail goes to an airport or a train yard. Airplanes and trains carry the mail fast and far. Trucks finish the trip to the post office.

At the post office, workers feed the mail
into a sorting machine. The machine
reads the bar codes. The bar codes
tell where the mail should be delivered.

Next, the machine sorts the mail into groups. Each letter carrier gets one group of mail. Handlers put the mail into bundles and sacks.

Letters carriers pick up the mail for their neighborhood. They deliver the mail every day except Sunday.

It's time to check the mail again. Did you get a letter? Say thanks to your community's postal workers.

Facts about Postal Workers

■ In the United States, mail is delivered by the U.S. Postal Service. This service is run by the national government. All postal workers work for the postal service.

■ About 700,000 people are postal workers in the United States.

■ United States postal workers deliver more than 200 billion pieces of mail every year! That's almost half the mail sent in the entire world.

■ Postal workers drive more than 210,000 trucks, cars, and vans to move all that mail.

■ Postal carriers bring mail to every single address in the United States. People can receive mail no matter where they live.

■ Mail is delivered by mule to Supai, Arizona. This small town in the Grand Canyon is at the bottom of cliffs that are too steep for trucks or cars!

Postal Workers through History

■ Hundreds of years ago, people hired messengers to carry mail. It could take weeks or months.

■ In America in 1775, Benjamin Franklin started the postal service that became the U. S. Postal Service. Its workers have delivered mail for more than 225 years. They have used horses, stagecoaches, steamboats, trains, trucks, and airplanes.

■ In 1861, the Pony Express delivered mail from the eastern United States to California in seven days. That was faster than ever before. Pony Express riders passed the mail from rider to rider so it never stopped moving.

■ Mail delivery has gotten much faster. The first mail delivery by airplane took place in 1911.

Glossary

bar code: tiny lines that a machine prints on mail to tell where it should be sent

clerk: a post office worker who takes letters from people

community: a group of people who live in the same city, town, or neighborhood. People in the same community usually share the same fire department, schools, libraries, and other helpful places.

delivering: carrying mail from one place to another

letter carrier: a worker who brings mail to homes and businesses, then picks up mail to be sent

mail: letters and packages that people send from one place to another

mail handler: workers who move mail from place to place at a post office

post office: a building where mail is sorted to be sent to different places

Index

About the Author

Shannon Knudsen writes and edits children's books. Her favorite kind of mail is magazines about movies and video games. She thanks the postal workers of Minneapolis, Minnesota, for delivering them.

Photo Acknowledgments

The photographs in this book appear courtesy of: © Sam Lund/Independent Picture Service, pp. 3, 12, 18, 27; © Tim Wright/CORBIS, p. 4; © Chris Hondros/Getty Images, pp. 5, 10; © Henry Diltz/CORBIS, p. 6; © AP| Wide World Photos, pp. 7, 8, 9, 15, 17, 23; © James Leynse/CORBIS, p. 11; © Jeff Topping/Getty Images, pp. 13, 19, 21, 24, 25; © William Gottlieb/CORBIS, p. 14; © Joe Raedle/Getty Images, p. 16; © Win McNamee/Getty Images, p. 20; © Reuters/CORBIS, p. 22; © Cathrine Wessel/CORBIS, p. 26; © Leonard de Selva/CORBIS, p. 29.
Front Cover: © Comstock Images.